YOUth Matters, Volume 1

YOUth Matters, Volume 1

Chancierra Coleman

Copyright © Chancierra Coleman 2023

ISBN: Softcover 978-1-941574-21-8

Library of Congress Control Number: 2023903310

Unless otherwise indicated, all Scripture quotations are taken from the Holy Bible, New Living Translation, copyright © 1996, 2004, 2015 by Tyndale House Foundation. Used by permission of Tyndale House Publishers, Carol Stream, Illinois 60188. All rights reserved.

Scripture quotations marked (CEV) are taken from the CONTEMPORARY ENGLISH VERSION, Copyright© 1995 by the American Bible Society. Used by permission.

Scripture quotations marked (ESV) are taken from THE HOLY BIBLE, ENGLISH STANDARD VERSION®, Copyright© 2001 by Crossway, a publishing ministry of Good News Publishers. Used by permission.

Scripture quotations marked (TLB) are taken from The Living Bible copyright © 1971. Used by permission of Tyndale House Publishers, Carol Stream, Illinois 60188. All rights reserved.

Contents and/or cover may not be reproduced or transmitted in whole or in part in any form or by any means electronic or mechanical, including photocopying, recording, or by any information storage and retrieval system without the express written consent of the publisher.

This book was printed in the United States of America.

To order additional copies of this book, contact:
cierracoleman828@gmail.com.

TABLE OF CONTENTS

Dedication	6
Acknowledgments	7
Introduction	8
Chapter 1: Your Thoughts Matter	9
Chapter 2: Your Emotions Matter	14
Chapter 3: Your Mental Health Matters	20
Chapter 4: Your Relationships Matter	28
Chapter 5: Your Education Matters	34
Chapter 6: Your Voice Matters	38
Chapter 7: Your Dreams, Plans, and Goals Matter	43

Dedication

This book is dedicated to every parent who is committed to being the best parent and role model that they can be, and it is dedicated to every child who desires to be loved, heard, and understood.

Acknowledgements

I am eternally grateful to God for the many talents and gifts He has given me. Writing a book is not only therapeutic for me, but it also allows me to form connections with many great people, some of who have played a major part in the process of creating this delightful book. I could not successfully have written this book without the guidance and help of a few others. Those people deserve to be publicly recognized.

I would like to thank Carla Gaskins and One Dominion Publishing for helping me with the publishing process from start to finish. She handled me with care and excellence and went above and beyond to present me with great opportunities, support, and time.

I would also like to thank Glenda Wright, my editor, for her patience, knowledge, skills, and diligence in working to provide a polished manuscript for all readers.

Last, I thank Geri Alicea for her time and effort in creating an amazing book cover and helping me to bring life to my vision for *YOUth Matters, Volume 1*.

Introduction

The parent-child relationship is the most important relationship we will ever have. This special bond affects the physical, emotional, and social development of the child and thus is the foundation for possibly every other relationship the child will have. Often this relationship creates the basis for the child's belief system and may affect who and what the child becomes. Parenting today is not like it has ever been in any other generation. Some of the basics will always remain the same, but children today need parenting on a whole other level because the world has changed so greatly even in the last five years.

YOUth Matters, Volume 1 was written to help bridge the gap between parents and children in this new era. Recognizing that not all traditional ways of parenting are always productive, I offer a different perspective and tips to parents who are receptive to applying different approaches when talking to, disciplining, and understanding their children on a different level. This book speaks to every parent and every child offering hope, change, and restoration in family dynamics while helping parents to destroy toxic parenting habits to help bring families closer together with love and understanding.

Chapter 1: Your Thoughts Matter

When you are an adolescent, life seems so unfair at times. You can speak and not be heard or communicate and not be understood. You can hurt, and it seems like no one cares. You can think, dream, and plan, only to be criticized and judged when you express those thoughts. You can be pushed to the back as if your thoughts, dreams, and plans are insignificant or not worthy enough to be recognized. The purpose of this book is to let you know that *you* matter! Everything about you matters! Your thoughts, emotions and feelings, your dreams, plans, goals, relationships, and your voice matters, even when you feel like they do not! I know exactly how it feels to be mistreated, overlooked, and counted out because I once felt the same way.

As a young girl with my own views about life, I felt very misunderstood, mistreated, and most of all rejected by family and friends who loved me unconditionally. It felt as if my thoughts and feelings did not matter to anyone. I was the type of child who no matter what someone said to me or about me would not allow their words to break me. What broke me was their actions towards me and the things they did to me. Although words did not affect me in some ways, the things that were said wounded my heart. Whoever said, "Sticks and stones may break my bones, but words will never hurt me" told a tall tale. Proverbs 18:21 tells us that what you say can preserve life or destroy it. That does not only apply to the person's life who speaks a thing, but it also applies to the person's life to whom they spoke it. There is power in your tongue! That is why you must be mindful of what comes out of your mouth about yourself and others. You can either pronounce blessings or curses out of your mouth. Words do hurt; they damage, they tear down, they destroy, and they kill.

YOUth Matters

As a child, I had to learn how to protect myself by developing "tough skin" as some would say. No one taught me how to protect myself against verbal and emotional abuse because in my case, it started in my household. Did you know that verbal/emotional abuse is defined as someone repeatedly using words to demean, frighten, or control someone? In other words, when people call you names, use words to shame you, speak down on you, humiliate, or downright criticize you, those are all signs of verbal/emotional abuse. It is not right, in any way, for a child to be susceptible to this type of abuse, especially in the comfort of their own home. From the time I left home to the time I arrived home from school, I was talked about and called out of my name. However, I never showed signs of weakness while being ridiculed. But in my private time, I cried with my face in my pillow. And after a while, I taught myself how to build a wall around the delicate parts of my innermost being so that no one else could hurt me.

I began to write about how I felt. I wrote daily, whether it was a good or dreadful day. Whatever the situation was, I wrote about it in my diaries. That was my way of expression. I had reached the point where I did not trust anyone enough to share my thoughts or the concerns of my heart. The closest people to me had broken that trust. It seemed as if I did not have a safe place, and to add insult to injury, I was so misunderstood by everyone around me. Not being able to express myself made me incredibly angry.

Note to parents:

What you speak into your child and about your children has the power to destroy them or build them up. You could be the reason your child grows up to be a broken adult all because you did not use your tongue to speak life, encourage, and empower them, but you used your tongue to demean, kill their character, break their spirit, and destroy them. Proverbs 14:1 says, "A wise woman builds her home, but a foolish woman tears it down with her own hands." Build do not destroy. Further, Ephesians 6:4 says, "Fathers, do not provoke your children to anger by the way you treat them." It is my belief that this Scripture is not gender specific, so it can be used for good parenting as inspired by Abba Father and indicates how to raise the children He has entrusted you with. If His Word says your children can be provoked, it means that you can be doing something wrong as a parent, and you are not always right.

After constantly being wronged, I began to build walls of protection inside my heart. I decided that overlooking mistreatment was the best option for me to move forward in life. My mindset was to protect my heart and mind at all costs, and it was reflected through my "oh well" attitude. The way I carried myself was not because I did not want to acknowledge what people said nor was it done out of fear. Instead, the best thing for me to do was to ignore what people thought of me. Since I could not change their opinions, why bother addressing it? In my mind, I wanted to tell people, "You can't talk to me like that," and I wanted to ask, "Why are you talking to me like that?" But I did not open my mouth. Children are typically limited in expressing themselves without the fear of being reprimanded. All I had was thoughts, thoughts that did not matter to anyone.

From being a young child all the way up until I was grown, my mother called me the "b" word repeatedly, as if it was my last name. The older I got, the angrier I became! Several years passed, and I still was not able to express my feelings to my mother. I dared not tell her what I thought about her as a parent and how it made me feel when she disrespected me. As I entered my mid-teens, I mustered up the boldness and courage to respond to her calling me that dreaded word again. I remember angrily expressing to her, "If I am one, then you're one!" The decision to stand up to my mother at that moment did not go so well. It was the first time I raised my fist to my mother after she jumped on me like I was a woman in the streets. Of course, in my mind, I was not trying to start a fight with my mother, but I wanted her to feel how I felt, low and disrespected. The years of not being able to express to her what I thought and what I felt when she mistreated me and verbally abused me pushed me to respond to her in a way that I was not proud of. The fifth commandment in Exodus 20:12 tells us to honor our father and our mother. There was no honor in what I said or did.

I am saying all of this to say expressing your thoughts matters! There is a way to express your feelings and still be respectful to your elders. Even as a child, sometimes you may have to be the "bigger person" and say, "Can I talk to you?" Expressing your feelings and thoughts simply means that you should be able to discuss what made you feel the way you felt based on your perspective of the situation. You can be free to express your thoughts once you learn how to deliver the message. Even if you are having the same problems amongst your peers, you can tell someone what you think about them without hurting their feelings or being disrespectful toward them. If they are unapproachable, then okay, continue your day as usual. You do not have to address every single issue, nor do you have to always say what is on your mind. Only express when necessary. Leave the rest to God. Use wisdom and know when it is time to speak and when to keep quiet. Your thoughts are powerful. What you think about yourself, others, and your life are valuable, and therefore, your thoughts matter!

YOUth Matters

Note to parents:

Parents, take a moment to re-evaluate your approach to your children. If you were your child, would you really consider yourself to be a safe space? Can they really trust you with their concerns, thoughts, and true feelings? Are you judgmental, unapproachable, or just inconsiderate of how they may feel?

I challenge you to write down three ways you can and will allow yourself to be more receptive to your child and their concerns.

_____
_____
_____
_____
_____
_____
_____
_____
_____
_____

Evaluations are necessary throughout life. Just like you want to be the best partner for your spouse, you should have the same desire to be the best parent for your child/children. How you make them feel really does matter.

Chapter 2: Your Emotions Matter

Many people use the words emotions and feelings interchangeably, but they are not exactly interchangeable terms. There is nothing specific that must happen for you to have emotions. Emotions are a gift from God, and He has emotions too! Your emotions are the control center for your feelings. If your emotional state is joyful, you may feel like crying, singing, cleaning, dancing, or laughing to express it. If your emotional state is sadness, you may feel the need to cry. Your emotions give you the ability to feel. What you feel determines the course of your actions. Therefore, it is extremely important to know how to manage your emotions and express your feelings in healthy ways.

As a young person, you typically grow up under the impression that girls are more emotional than boys. That is not true! We all have emotions; it is just more common for females to be more open and outwardly expressive about what they feel. For some reason, young men, typically young Black men, are raised to be tough, and they are not encouraged to express their feelings. If a young boy cries, someone in his family will usually tell him to stop crying or to stop acting like a girl. If his peers are around, they will call him demeaning names or attack his character because he expresses himself in a way that society deems as abnormal. What we should be told is to feel what you feel and let it go.

No one has the right to invalidate what you feel or how you feel. What this means is that no one should deny, reject, or dismiss your feelings! Your feelings matter! You have the right to express yourself if you are not causing any harm or disrespect to anyone when doing so. It may seem like you cannot verbally communicate how you feel. It is okay to write them down. If you do not want to write, find another positive way to express what you feel. You may be an artist; if so, draw your feelings out. If you are a dancer, find a song and choreograph a dance. Writing poetry, a song, or a rap may be your means of expressing how you feel. Whatever helps you to release, do it. The only wrong way to express how you feel is to harm yourself or someone else. Even when you pray, which is talking to God, it is okay to tell Him that you are upset, angry, sad, disgusted, or whatever you may be experiencing at that moment. He understands! He created you! He wants you to feel. He wants you to be expressive. It is normal!

When I got in trouble as a young child, my mother disciplined me. She used her hand along with whatever object she could find whether it was a shoe or belt to hit me. Afterwards, she would stand by and wait for my reaction. My siblings would immediately burst into tears and cry aloud. I was the one who just stood and looked at my mom, waiting for it to be over. She would say things like, "So you just gonna stand there and not cry huh? Okay, I am gonna keep whooping you till you cry then." And guess what I would do after a few more licks? I would start crying.

Weird, right? Well, I did not cry in the beginning because I did not want her to see that she was hurting me. That is how a lot of young men learn how to process their feelings, especially when they are hurt. They grow older and must develop a tough shell on the outside so that people will not think they are weak, all while they are crying on the inside. You are not weak for expressing your feelings young man, but you become weak when you do not express yourself. No matter how strong you try to be, the weight of suppressed feelings from neglecting to properly deal with those emotions can cause you to fall.

No emotion is a bad emotion, not even anger. The Word of God says, "Be angry and do not sin; do not let the sun go down on your anger and give no opportunity to the devil" (Ephesians 4:26-27, ESV). This shows that you have the right to be angry, and this is not a terrible thing. What can be bad about this emotion is what comes from it, which are the negative thoughts and actions you act out to express your anger. You should not allow anger to set in your heart. Feel what you feel, and let it go. It may not be as simple as one, two, three. It may take a few minutes or longer, but do not allow it to stay and build up in your heart.

When it comes to expressing yourself to your elders, be respectful. Just because knowing what you think and how you feel is important, it does not give you permission to be disrespectful. And being a young person does not give an adult permission to disrespect you. Yes parents, you can be disrespectful to your children, and it is not right. Even something that you may think is simple like smoking in front of them is a sign of disrespect. As a child, one of the things I disliked that made me terribly upset was when adults smoked in the house or in the car while I was with them. I could not say, "I don't like you smoking around me," or "I feel violated when you..." because as a child I heard adults say how grown they were and that they could do whatever they wanted to do. Instead of saying what was on my mind and telling them how that made me feel, I could not do anything besides be mad.

Note to parents:

An answer is not an explanation. The attitude of "I don't have to explain myself to a child" is a bad attitude to have. If you asked a child an open-ended question and they responded without an explanation, you would not be satisfied. It is the same when they ask you a question. You must understand that, oftentimes, children ask questions not to question your authority but for clarity and understanding. Your response may just stop them from making the same mistakes or decisions you made if you give an answer and explanation to help them understand clearly, which in turn increases their knowledge. Remember, "A kind answer soothes angry feelings, but harsh words stir them up"

(Proverbs 15:1, CEV). If your child asks a question or states how something makes them feel, do not belittle them or invalidate their feelings. Be understanding and respond respectfully. They are human too.

It is important and helpful for you to process your feelings outwardly. Forget about what people will think of you for speaking out and expressing yourself. Boy, girl, man, or woman, we are all created in the image of God (Genesis 1:27). We all have equal rights to feel and communicate those feelings. He cares for you (1 Peter 5:7), and He wants you to know that your emotions and feelings matter!

Questions for Parents:

As a parent who was once a child, take a moment to recall how some adults made you feel disrespected by word or deed. What was said or done and how did it make you feel?

_____
_____
_____
_____
_____
_____
_____

Have you taken into consideration any of those things that you did not like to be done to you or in front of you so that you understand how you may make your child(ren) feel sometimes?

_____
_____
_____
_____
_____
_____
_____

In what ways do you let your child(ren) know that their emotions and feelings are important to you?

_____
_____
_____
_____
_____
_____
_____

Questions for Youth:

What are some emotions you are feeling now? Why?

_____
_____
_____
_____
_____
_____

When you are hurt, upset, or feeling an emotion you do not like to feel, whether it stems from an issue at home or school, how do you manage those emotions?

_____
_____
_____
_____
_____
_____

If you want to be understood, sometimes you may have to explain yourself. I challenge you to respectfully share your emotions and how you feel often with your parents or some trusted source. What can you share now?

_____
_____
_____
_____
_____
_____

Chapter 3: Your Mental Health Matters

I was taught that an idle mind is the enemy's playground. If you have an idle mind, you have allowed room for the enemy to infiltrate your mind, causing you to entertain those negative thoughts that lead you to inevitably act on what you are thinking possibly in a negative way. For you not to act out those types of thoughts, you need to have good self-control and feed your mind with things that are worthy of thinking about and entertaining. This is a major key concerning your mental health because your mental health matters!

By the time a child makes it to elementary school, they are already equipped with what they need to show respect for themselves and others. They know what is right and what is wrong according to the level they are on, and as they grow, they learn more. At a certain age, you are responsible and accountable for how you conduct yourself whether in school or at home. The Center for Disease Control says that mental health affects how we think, feel, and act. If you are not healthy psychologically, then it will show emotionally and socially; therefore, it is important for you to maintain a healthy balance amongst the three.

How do you develop and maintain good mental health? I advise you to first and foremost develop a relationship with God. Studying Scripture and praying is how I learned to maintain a good state of mind, yes, even as a young child. If I did, you can too. In the Bible, Ecclesiastes 12:1 says, "Don't let the excitement of youth cause you to forget your Creator. Honor Him in your youth before you grow old." You can honor Him in thought, the things you say and do, by seeking Him for direction or comfort, talking with Him, and putting Him first in all you do. According to Isaiah 26:3, when you keep Him and His Word on your mind, He keeps you in perfect peace. In this way, there is very little space for the enemy to play games with your mind.

I understand there are things that happen in life that will cause you to be unhappy, doubtful, scared, hurt, confused, anxious, sad, or angry, but there are some things you can do to make sure you do not stay stuck in those emotional states. Remember, we want to be in good health, not just physically but mentally. How you are mentally is influenced by your environment, the people you are surrounded by, and the things you consistently see and experience.

Here are 10 keys to developing and protecting your mental health:

- Pray

    Use this space to write a prayer about some things you want God to help you with.

    _____
    _____
    _____
    _____
    _____
    _____
    _____
    _____
    _____
    _____
    _____
    _____
    _____
    _____
    _____

- Connect with good people and create positive friendships.

Make a list of people you consider to be "good" people.

Explain how you can create positivity in your family relationships and friendships.

_____
_____
_____
_____
_____
_____
_____
_____
_____
_____
_____
_____
_____
_____
_____

- Think positive thoughts. Every child of God has the power to take captive every thought to make it obedient to Christ (2 Cor. 10:5). You do not have to entertain those negative thoughts. His Word tells us what things we should think about in Philippians 4:8.

Write down at least five positive "I Am" affirmations about yourself!

YOUth Matters

_____

- Engage in physical activity. Most people find that working out or exercising is a stress reliever. It makes you feel better in body and mind.

What types of physical activities do you enjoy engaging in? What are some activities you want to try?

_____

- Be openly expressive about things that bother you. Keeping quiet and not expressing how you feel and what you may be experiencing internally is not good for your health. We all need and should have someone we can talk to, even if you must speak with a counselor or therapist. Let it out.

CHALLENGE: I challenge you to have a conversation with someone about your feelings about a situation, then write about how you think the conversation went.

_____
_____
_____
_____
_____
_____
_____
_____
_____
_____
_____
_____

- Set goals, then focus and work to accomplish them.

Start now by writing down 3-5 realistic, short goals that you want to accomplish.

_____
_____
_____
_____
_____
_____

- Be confident in who you are and have good self-esteem. This means that no matter what negative things anyone ever says about you, do not allow them to kill your spirit, your hope, or steal your peace. Stay true to yourself.

What does having confidence and good self-esteem look like for you?

YOUth Matters

- Be an optimist, a person who tends to be hopeful and confident about the future or the success of something. Speak no negativity.

    What negative things do you need to delete from your vocabulary?
    _____
    _____
    _____
    _____
    _____
    _____

- Listen to encouraging music. If you are mad, you probably should not listen to a rap song that is talking about shooting up a club or hurting someone. Your ears are gates and what you allow to go into them can settle in your heart. Listen to music that speaks life to you and uplifts you.

    What are some of your favorite songs right now? Are they encouraging and uplifting to your spirit?
    _____
    _____
    _____
    _____
    _____

YOUth Matters

_____
_____
_____
_____
_____
_____
_____
_____
_____

- Focus on the things you can control. Never allow things, situations, or the decisions of others who are out of your control to make you feel guilty of anything.

Name the things you can control.

_____
_____
_____
_____
_____
_____

If you are not healthy mentally, you are no good for yourself or anyone else. Assess your mental health and recognize when you may need help. There is someone near who you can trust with those things concerning you. You just have to be willing to share.

Chapter 4: Your Relationships Matter

The word relationship is defined as the state of being connected. To be connected means you are joined together to provide access and communication between two or more people. The connections that join you together in a relationship with others matter! Having discernment and listening to wisdom can save you a lifetime of troubles and heartbreak. I know it can be embarrassing for whatever reason to let your friends and peers meet your parents, but most of the time, your parents know when a person means good for you. It is not wise for you to form relationships or friendships with others outside of your parents' knowledge. Because your relationships matter, you need to know how to have healthy ones.

The first relationships we form and are aware of are those within our family. Our family is how we learn the foundational principles on which we build on throughout life concerning all other relationships. These relationships should teach us how to love, listen, communicate effectively, and connect with others outside of our family and should teach us to set a standard as to how we should be loved, treated, and talked to. Your family does not just want to be in your "business," but more than likely, they care. They care about you and the people you connect to because not all connections are good connections. Your parents care because they know the dangers of the world and the dangers of being in a relationship with the wrong people.

The most meaningful relationship to have in your life is with the Lord your God. Jesus said in Mark 12:30, "You must love the Lord your God with all your heart, all your soul, all your mind, and all your strength." This is the first commandment. Being a Christian, a follower of Christ, is not about religion. It is clearly about having a relationship with God. You must know Him and

His Word for yourself. The relationship is personal. He knows you, and you must get to know Him. He loves you, and He wants you to have healthy relationships. Even the second commandment tells us to love your neighbor as yourself. Jesus said, "No other commandment is greater than these" (Mark 12:31). So, you see, relationships are important to God. He wants us to love and treat one another right.

The most popular type of relationships being praised and laughed at these days are "toxic" relationships. Some think it is normal for a guy to hurt a woman or for a woman to hurt a guy or even for "friends" to talk bad to or about each other. That type of behavior is not normal, funny, or cute, and it is not love. To intentionally inflict harm upon someone, whether physically or verbally, is an act of hate. You do not treat people you love disrespectfully. You should always think about how you would feel or what you would do if someone treated you or talked to you the way you may talk to or treat others.

When I was a younger girl, I witnessed my mother, who was involved in a toxic relationship, get physically and verbally abused for years. Sometimes, I had to pull him off her or yell and stand in the way, preventing him from hitting her or so they would stop fighting. I did not like it. However, I assumed in my mind that they loved each other because he would always come back around after these detrimental incidents. They were always okay until the next episode. I did not know what caused the fights each time they happened, but for some reason, I never judged him for fighting my mother in front of my siblings and me. It was not until I got a little older that I started to realize that my mother played a part in this toxic relationship. I noticed that sometimes she said and did things to provoke him into anger. She verbally disrespected him and periodically destroyed his belongings. There were several times when my siblings and I sensed that something bad was about to happen and begged our mother to just be quiet or to leave him alone. In some cases, he tried to walk away from her to avoid confrontation, and she followed him, still cursing him. Before we knew it, they were fighting. As a child, how can you stop two people who are quick to anger? It was something we just had to deal with. That relationship was not a good one for my mother, and it was not a good example for us of how people should love one another. You must know that your decisions to be in unhealthy relationships do not only affect you and that person, but they affect your family and the people closest to you.

In the old days, young men had to go to the father and family of the young woman they were interested in dating or marrying to get the family's approval. I think people should go back to those ways. Allow them to meet your people before you run off and fall head over hills in love. Save your love and body for the one who deserves it. Sad is the day you get deceived and hurt then end up with your face in a pillow crying because you moved too soon.

My baby sister started dating this guy during her senior year in high school. When some of the members in our family recognized who he was, we told her he was not a good guy for her. Being young and naïve and thinking they were "in love," she continued seeing him. She began making unwise decisions and getting herself caught up in things she had no business being involved in. Within a matter of months, things started to get intense between them. We talked to her, prayed with her and for her, and tried to encourage her to do better. She finally reached the point where she thought she was ready to leave him alone, then she found out she was pregnant. She continued talking to and seeing him even though he was abusing her. She was now caught up in the same cycle our mother and grandmother once went through.

One day when she was a few months pregnant, he fought her, and she tried to leave him when one of our family members came to her rescue. As she tried to leave him, he shot her. He went to jail for a little while, but when he was released, they reconnected. She thought he "changed" and that he really loved her and their child. So, she took a chance at being a family, allowing him to actively be around for his daughter's sake. Not listening to her family and thinking that she knew who he was cost her a far greater price this time around. She was already at a point of no return, but she finally decided to leave him for good. This guy was controlling, abusive, and a menace to society. He wanted to alienate her and get her to a point where she had nothing or nobody to help or try to save her.

She never felt safe with him, but because he always threatened her and it seemed like he could not be stopped, she felt as if she was forced to deal with him. Every time he abused her, he was released from jail. If he wanted to see his daughter, he used that reason to hold her captive mentally. She decided to finally move on with her life, and she strategically left him. Within a week after leaving him, he tragically killed her in front of my niece, his child. I lost my sweet, beautiful, twenty-one-year-old sister on June 15, 2022 to the same type of domestic violence our mother and grandmother were once involved in. The only difference is that they made it out of those relationships, but unfortunately, she did not.

That is one reason why it is extremely important for you to listen to the voice of those who care about you when it comes to creating new connections and relationships. Your relationships matter, not just for females but also for males. Your mother or someone close to you will be able to tell you if someone is right for you. Those with discernment around you will tell you the dangers of socializing and hanging around with certain people and crowds, even your friends who you think are so cool. God put people in place to see *for* you when you may not be able to see. Sometimes, there are things about a person you will not see until it is too late. Why waste your time, energy, and love on someone who is not right for you? Listen to wisdom! You will not miss any good thing that is for you. You do not have to rush or be pressured into any relationship. Just wait, use good judgement, and be willing to listen to the people who have your best interests at heart. Create and maintain healthy, beneficial relationships. You do not want to be unequally yoked, out of tune, and out of order because you are in relationship with the wrong people (2 Corinthians 6:14).

Here are three tell-tale signs of toxic behaviors in parent-child relationships, as well as friendships and future romantic relationships:

1. Any form of abuse: verbal, sexual, mental, physical, or emotional.
2. A jealous and controlling person.

This person does not want you to have healthy and genuine friendships/relationships with other people. They may try to control who you talk to, where you go, what you wear, what you do and how you do it. They tend to get mad when you do not listen to them and only them and when you do not do what they want you to do. You can have friends who act this way toward you. If that friend makes you feel bad all of the time or always mistreats you, you should probably not want to be connected to that person. How someone makes you feel matters and if you tell them how their behavior makes you feel and they continue to behave the same way, you should understand, that is who they are, and you cannot change them. You can only change how you deal with them.

3. A person who will not accept accountability.

This person will typically blame everything on you all of the time in every situation. They never admit to their wrongdoing, and they make you feel guilty for whatever the problem is. In the parent-child relationship all of these things are included as well. Other unhealthy signs include selfishness, violent behavior, being unsupportive, provocative, emotionally immature- taking their emotions out on their children over issues they may have had at work or within their other relationships.

Think about your relationship with your family and your friends. How would you describe a "toxic" relationship?

_____
_____
_____
_____
_____
_____
_____

How do you know if a friendship or relationship is healthy or unhealthy?

_____
_____
_____
_____
_____
_____
_____

Chapter 5: Your Education Matters

I am sure your parents talk to you about staying in school and going on to college, and you have even asked the question, "Why do I have to go to school or attend college?" The answer they gave you was, "Because you need an education." That is true. Your education matters! You may not understand how much it matters now, but you will in time. You may not agree with taking all the classes you have to take or fully understand why you need to take them. Trust me! I had the same thoughts and attitude about education when I was in high school. I expressed several times that certain classes had nothing to do with what I wanted to do after completing high school. I asked, "Why do I have to learn all these formulas for math if I am not going to use them after this class...? It is so stupid!" I felt like I never got the right answers.

As I grew older and really knew what career I wanted to have, I realized that for the career I chose, I had to have my high school diploma and at least a bachelor's degree if I wanted to be qualified to do the work, I dreamed of doing. There is a difference between flipping burgers for the rest of your life and hiring people to flip the burgers. Or even better, there is a difference between being a manager or supervisor at a burger joint or the owner of the burger spot! The difference is the levels of education. Granted, no matter what you decide to do, make it your business to do it to the best of your ability! Hard work does pay off, but if you want to go where the real money is, you have to level up, and it all starts with your knowledge and education!

I cannot express to you enough how pertinent it is for you to be educated. Lack of education affects your life in so many ways. Not only do you need to be educated but you also need an understanding of what you are being taught. Your education does not stop at school. You should be a student throughout your lifetime until the day you leave this earth. It is foolish to think you know everything there is to know. This is why you must be teachable and coachable. You should live to learn something new every day, always willing to receive knowledge, wisdom, and understanding. Proverbs 4:7 tells us that, "Wisdom is the principal thing; Therefore, get wisdom and in all thy getting, get an understanding." It is great to receive knowledge and wisdom, but it is even greater for you when you receive an understanding because then you will apply what you know to your daily life.

I am aware of the many distractions that may occur while you are in school. The greatest distraction is, drum roll please, those of the opposite sex. Yes! For young men, the young women are distractions. For young women, the young men are distractions. Your focus should be on being great, passing your classes, and earning every credit so that you can be promoted and graduate on time! If you are involved in any extracurricular activities, let those activities occupy your mind outside of class so that you can have a better chance at staying out of trouble or being caught up entertaining those "boyfriend/girlfriend" distractions. It is necessary to form friendships and bonds with people we can trust. The mistake many of us make is looking for love in all the wrong places at the wrong time.

Do not get me wrong! I know it is fun to date and text while you are smiling from ear to ear and to have someone to stay up late on the phone with while falling asleep still holding the phone and waking up early in the morning ready to get to school to see them! Yeah, I know! You want to be cute and cool walking down the hallways together, holding hands, taking pictures together, and doing all the things you think you should be doing, but you can quickly get sidetracked and heartbroken when you do not understand that it is all fun and games. Rarely will you find a guy in high school who will date a female because he is looking for his wife. Of course, there are many people who say they found the love of their life in high school; they call them "high school sweethearts." But just because it is possible for you, your attention should be placed more on your education as you prepare for your future. Allowing yourself to get caught up in this type of distraction can impact you for the rest of your life.

Questions for Youth

What are some careers you have in mind?

_____
_____
_____
_____
_____
_____

Do you know how many years of education are needed beyond high school to enter the career you desire?

_____
_____
_____
_____
_____
_____

What are some things you love doing that you would do even if you did not get paid for it? In other words, what are you passionate about?

_____
_____
_____
_____
_____
_____

Chapter 6: Your Voice Matters

Do you get in trouble for talking too much, or are you too shy to speak? Maybe you fit somewhere in between the two. Whichever side you identify with, there is a reason. It could be that you are innately talkative and were encouraged to be open in expressing yourself. It could be that you stopped talking so much because you were always told to be quiet, or you are shy and lack confidence to speak, which caused you to live in your shell. Whatever the reason, I want you to know that your voice does matter.

While it is good to talk, you should not talk as much as you listen. We have two ears and one mouth for a reason. Talking too much usually means you are listening too little. There is a time to talk and a time to keep quiet. Let us use the school setting for example. If your teacher is giving you step-by-step instructions on how to complete a classwork assignment and you are having a side conversation, are you talking at the right or wrong time? You can avoid trouble if you are able to discern the time and control your tongue.

What about talking too much at home? Here is another example – is it the right or wrong time to voice your thoughts and opinions when your parent or guardian is talking to you or reprimanding you for something you have done? Verbalizing how you feel in that moment made it into an unnecessary discussion when they were trying to make a statement or give you a command. In cases like these, you are talking at the wrong time.

Proverbs 21:23 tells us "Watch your tongue and keep your mouth shut and you will stay out of trouble." That does not mean to be quiet all the time; it simply means to be cautious and mindful of when you should speak, and when you do, be mindful of what you say. You must use wisdom to know and understand when it is your time to speak, using your voice to speak respectfully. If there is a situation where you feel like you want to speak to an adult, approach them respectfully. Most times you can do it alone, but if you think you may need another adult present, then handle it that way. But you can ask, "Can I talk to you?" about whatever the problem is. You do not start "going off."

One of my younger sisters used to get in trouble often because she loved to talk. She talked so much, people nicknamed her Channel 5, a news reporting station, or they called her Oprah, who was a talk show host. She was the child who thought she had all the information, and in her eyes if something happened, it was meant to be told. If something was said, it was worth being repeated. She sometimes put an extra spin to what she tried to repeat, fabricating the truth. Even after my mother repeatedly told us not to tell what was going on in our household, my sister could not hold her tongue. She got in trouble at home, and she got in trouble in school. She talked so much she would tell on herself and others too. She went to sleep and woke up talking. Everyone in the house knew that when she came home from school, she was coming in with a story.

She always had something to talk about, but I never witnessed anyone nurture her gift of speaking, instead she was usually in hot water. She was called names such as messy, liar, and drama queen. Although most of the time she told the truth, people did not like her telling their business, so they tried to silence her voice by telling others she was not to be considered credible or was impossible to believe. It can be very hurtful when you are a child and no one believes anything you say, especially when your parent(s) is responsible for telling others you are a liar, ruining your reputation rather than protecting your image and teaching you how to use your voice.

YOUth Matters

Note to parents:

It is your responsibility to see the gifts and potential within your child so that you can nurture and cultivate them. A talkative child could seem bad naturally, but your child could very well be a mouthpiece to be used by God. Because your child is not equipped spiritually and taught how they should use their mouth, they end up using their gift the best way they naturally know how, and that is not always good. When your child is gifted to speak and prophesy, you must be their eyes and recognize that at an early age, the enemy will try to pervert the gift and cancel the assignment, calling, and purpose God has for them. He will make your child out to be a liar to you and others.

Yes, your child may say the first thing that comes to mind and may tell people about themselves without regret. They may tell all your business and may not know when to speak and when not to speak, but that is why they must be trained early. Do not silence the voice of your child. Be patient and ask God for guidance on how to deal with your child. Never speak negatively! You could be speaking a word curse over their gift or planting a seed that you will later have to uproot. Your words are powerful. Speak life and positivity into your kid's life. Speak not of what you see but of that which you want to see. You do not always have to tell your family, friends, and coworkers what your child is struggling with. Protect them by keeping them before God and allow Him to do His work in them, and He will place the people your child needs in their life to help fulfill their purpose.

Now, concerning those of you who are shy and really do not like to talk much, I encourage you to come out of that shell. Being shy and fearful, lacking confidence, and boldness will cost you. You could miss so many opportunities because you do not want to open your mouth. I am sure you have heard, "A closed mouth doesn't get fed." It is true. How can you expect people to know what you need, what you want, what is bothering you, how you feel, or what you dislike if you do not use your voice?

There are people in the world that will treat you any kind of way, walk over you, look past you, leave you out, and push you off if you do not know how to speak up for yourself. Your voice matters in so many ways, but if you do not use it, you will never know the difference you can make. I leave you with this Scripture, Joshua 1:9, "Be strong and courageous. Do not be afraid and do not panic before them. For the Lord, your God will personally go ahead of you. He will never leave you nor forsake you." Whenever it is your time to speak, open your mouth and be free. Respectfully.

Tips: **Speak Up, Speak Out**

- It is not always what you say, It is how you say it.

- You cannot speak to adults in the same way you would talk to your peers. There is a certain level of respect you should have when expressing yourself to your elders. Be mindful of that.

- Think before you speak.

- Be honest and speak your truth with respect.

- Every thought is not worth expressing. Learn what to say and when to say it.

- If you are not a talker, explore other ways your voice can be heard.

Chapter 7: Your Goals Matter

Have you ever wondered how or why we have an imagination? One reason is because God allows us to see a glimpse of what He wants to do in our lives. He wants you to be able to see it and develop a strong enough faith to obtain what you see according to His will. In other words, He wants you to use your imagination to paint a picture of your future. God knew exactly who you were and what you are going to do in life before He created you (Jeremiah 1:5). Before you even grow old enough to make plans or goals for yourself and before you are birthed into the world to your parents, God already has plans for you. In Jeremiah 29:11 in The Living Bible, God tells us, "For I know the plans I have for you. Plans for good and not for evil. To give you a future and a hope." If God has plans for you, He wants you to be aligned with the will and plan He has for your life. That is why your dreams, goals, and plans matter!

You have created short-term and long-term goals before, right? If you have not, you are going to start! Writing goals down and accomplishing them is rewarding. I started writing goals down when I was in elementary school. To this day, I still write down goals. There is a method I like to use when writing goals now, and I learned this from my coach when I was studying to receive my life coaching certification. The method is called S.M.A.R.T. To be intentional about the goals you create, they should be **S**pecific, **M**easurable (I am going from this to that), **A**ttainable (achievable within a reasonable amount of time), **R**ealistic, **T**imely (have deadlines). Sometimes, things in life happen that can cause us to stagger or fall behind on accomplishing goals when we intend to, but God's timing is perfect, and if it is His will, we can still accomplish those goals. His Word in Isaiah 60:22 says, "When the time is right I, the Lord, will make it happen."

YOUth Matters

The Bible tells us in Proverbs 16:9, "We can make our plans, but the Lord determines our steps." A few chapters later, Proverbs 19:21 says, "You can make many plans, but the Lord's purpose will prevail." You have power to speak or plan for yourself, but God has the final say. He is your GPS, and He uses His God Positioning System throughout the course of fulfilling those goals and plans to get you where you are supposed to be according to His time and purpose for you. I made many plans concerning my career, when I would get married, what kind of house I would live in, what kind of cars I would drive, and several other things in my life, but I had to use His GPS to get what He had for me. Everything did not turn out how I thought, but the results were most times better than I could have wanted or asked for. Making plans and goals allows you to use your imagination and allows God to reveal to you what He has in store for you. Make plans. Make goals. Pray and follow Jesus.

One of my most recent goals was to complete this book for you within seven days. With no help, no one to hold me accountable, no one to motivate me to keep me going, I had to be my own motivation. I had to want to accomplish this goal more than anything else. I had to remain focused, dedicated, determined, and committed to my goal to finish it on time. I did it all while being a young, widowed mother to five children, and living and maintaining a remarkably busy life and schedule. I had to sacrifice what I wanted to do. I could have been selfish. I could have been a procrastinator. I could have even directed my focus and attention to several other areas in my life, but I decided to set a goal, and I had to stick with it no matter what. Yes, I was tired. Yes, I still had to cook. Yes, I still had to clean. Yes, I still had to tend to my children. Yes, I still had to work. Yes, I still had to take care of business. Yes, there were many distractions, and life did not stop because I had things to accomplish. I had to make some temporary adjustments to complete the task at hand. Sooner than later, I knew things would be worth it. That is the type of attitude you must have when you want to achieve greatness. Work at it and do not stop until it is done.

You can create and define your own future. Do not leave that power in the hands of anyone else. Think about what you want. Speak what you want. Write what you want. See yourself having what you want. Work for what you want, and soon, what you want is going to be what you have. You must take delight in the Lord, and He will give you your heart's desires (Psalm 34:7). Find joy in Him so much so that no matter what goes your way or does not go your way, you will still be satisfied with Him and full of joy.

No goal is too small. A goal is simply something that needs to be done. Recognize what it is and do it. The power to get it done lies within you. It is good to have an accountability partner, someone who can stand by you along the way, pushing you to get it done. But even if you do not have one, it is possible for you to reach your mark. Use your imagination. Think big. Dream big. Plan, pray, and execute because it all matters!

What are three short-term goals you want to accomplish?

_____
_____
_____
_____
_____
_____
_____

What are three long-term goals you want to accomplish?

_____
_____
_____
_____

_____
_____

For each goal, you must know how you will achieve it. What are you going to do to ensure that you work diligently at accomplishing each goal?

_____
_____
_____
_____
_____
_____

Who or what do you need in order to execute your plans?

_____
_____
_____
_____
_____
_____

No matter what your dreams, plans, and goals are, remember that they matter, and you are destined for greatness! Believe in yourself, work diligently, and you will be rewarded. May all of your dreams come true according to the will of God.

Biography

Chancierra is the eldest child of her mother's six children. She grew up fatherless, in poverty, and had to learn quickly how to be responsible as she assisted her young, single parent with siblings and bills during her early teen years. At the age of sixteen, she gave birth to her first child. By the time she graduated high school, she was a single parent of two. She continued her education and became a medical assistant.

At age twenty-five, she got married. In August of 2021, she unexpectedly lost her mother to COVID pneumonia. Nine days after losing her mother and six days before her sixth wedding anniversary, her husband and brother-in-law were murdered on the same night. She was left a broken, motherless widow of four at age thirty-one.

Shortly after these events, she immediately went forth pursuing her purpose, becoming a certified life coach, and releasing her first book, *PUSH*.

In May 2021, she graduated from Georgia State University receiving her first degree. The death of her sister a month later due to domestic violence pushed her to officially start a nonprofit for youth called All Youth Matter, Inc. This organization stands as the voice for youth up to twenty-one years old. Its mission is to encourage, empower, coach, inspire, and support youth and young adults through whatever they face daily.

Chancierra is a woman of God, psalmist, entrepreneur, author, youth advocate, and life coach.

YOUth Matters

Information

For information on All Youth Matter, Inc, coaching, or other inquiries contact her at: cierracoleman828@gmail.com.

www.ingramcontent.com/pod-product-compliance
Lightning Source LLC
Chambersburg PA
CBHW042112120526
44592CB00042B/2789